A Chair
at the Café

For Mary, without whose help
this would not have happened

And my children
Marie, Chris and Andrew

Crumps Barn Studio
No.2 The Waterloo, Cirencester GL7 2PZ
www.crumpsbarnstudio.co.uk

Cover design by Lorna Gray

Printed in the UK by Severn, Gloucester on responsibly sourced paper

MIX
Paper from
responsible sources
FSC® C022174

ISBN 978-1-915067-30-2

A Chair
at the Café

HILDA COCHRANE

Collected Poems

Crumps Barn Studio

SPAIN

SUNRISE OVER CALPE

I am an eagle in my eyrie;
On high I sense the rising sun
yet unseen; her hidden presence
brings colour; crimson artistry
running the length of horizon,
lighting up the city-shaped clouds,
stretching out to tint sleeping town.
Trailing her gown, distilling red,
she slides into glorious tints,
rose-pink folds softly into amber.
High Ifach stands proudly jewelled
by this golden goddess of dawn,
brightly she rises; the world wakes,
dawn sleeps, paled by her vital fire.

FRANCE

A CHAIR AT THE CAFÉ

Immobilised,
In this chair;
others bustling,
laughing, lively,
knock at its wheels,
scrape their heels
on its metal rods.
They glare
at my carer

she stares,
indifferent;
anchors my chariot,
straightens wraps
around my creased body;
still-faced, impassive,
claps for a waiter:
Coke and *chocolat chaud;*
tacit silence

between us,
inevitability,
words unspoken;
loneliness
forgotten:
Coke and *chocolat chaud;*
a token
to salve
painful remembrance

ACACIA

Acacia, cream pendants
of elegant blossoms;
rampant at the edge of
meadow, lane and field.

Our laden senses yield
to the rich fragrance of
lacy floral clusters;
then comes a fluster, a

stir of zephyr breezes
loosening the petals,
freeing them, lifting them,
twirling them at leisure

in delicate drifts.
A floating, floral, snow
paving untrodden paths
with sweet-scented treasure.

METAMORPHOSIS

The night-owl sat upon the floor,
he read a while, then read some more;
the daylight fled, night came instead
but never did he seek his bed.

He knew of plots and fairy things,
of hate, of peace, and magickings;
in time the words gave him a look
resembling a well-read book.

His eyes and mouth were 'ahs' and 'ohs',
the letter 'T' his brows and nose;
his back grew flat and very fine,
like ridges on a good book's spine.

His fingers flattened crisp and svelte,
Like the pages of a novelette;
squiggles replaced his face … and squirms;
learnéd signs of confirmed bookworms

MONOCHROME MAN

On the path, steadily, heavily,
comes monochrome man;
gloom in the morning sunshine,
an eye to the sky:
'It will rain today'

It will rain, it will snow,
The north winds do blow
in his colourless head.

By his side, merrily, cheerily,
wild flowers dazzle;
velvet yellow gaiety
whispering to catch
his clouded eye.

It's raining, it's pouring,
this man should be snoring
in his dull bed.

In the field, joyfully, musically,
a brown lark rises,
dips and soars; a rapture
to capture his ear;
he does not hear.

He is deep in the puddle,
Right up to his middle;
quite cold and quite numb.

Leave him clouded in gloom,
let his buttercups fade;
let his lark become dumb,
leave him
stumbling and blind
in the rags of his mind,
a beggar in town —
two-dimensionally grim,
cardboard thin
is monochrome man.

DEVON

A DEVON DAY

Some days the seas are leaden grey,
a view obscured, a hiding sun;
sometimes those tears of drizzling rain
wink briefly while they slowly plane
down aimless tracks of waterways
treading my window; damp tremblings
twinkling, gliding, then diverging;
running in rivers or merging
with each other, slipping, sliding …

beyond, a charcoal sea is set
to let white wavelets pirouette

a smiling hint of sudden sun
has breezed right in, clouds disappear;
streams of light thrust gloom away,
a rainbow bends, a perfect sphere
casts sky blue tints to calm the sea;
azure now stains the foamy waves,
a brightness spurs our shining hearts,
a happy sense of flying free …

Now aquamarine paints the sea,
as white-foam wavelets dance with glee.

HURRICANE

Drumbeats threaten, a fierce warning, a din
of noise; gales gust, a whiplash of cruel rain
against the windowpane. We are entombed;
all doors, all outlets closed in a vain hope,
a need to cope, withstand ferocity.
Bullying winds shriek, shatter barriers,
Slam into the walls; foundations shaking
as these harriers bluster, bleed through cracks.

Trees, plants, quake at such animosity,
battered branches sag, sway, bend, to earth's floor
in urgent need of age-old defenses.
No blackbird flits in song, the cawing crow
has fled. A safe place, shaded, dark?
        We don't know.

EAST-THE-WATER

East-The-Water offers the sign *Instow*
Yelland, with the hint of fine yellow sands;
an inland estuary breaks free from the sea,
a river, moving, forever changing
awaits the tide which rushes in, then ebbs
revealing webbed ridges. Stranded boats
hover, impatient to have high water
scurry, flurry around and make them spin.

Maybe the sun gleams, perhaps rain may fall,
but nothing alters the will of ocean.
The motions of time still hold their rhythm,
can climb high on moon-paths they are given;
the heavens know when to drop those crafts down,
then send in a flood, set them crowned on high
to woo the spell-bound watchers passing by
Yelland, East-The-Water, Instow.

IN REVERENCE

She was looking, starved of leisure,
for reference to a Browning text.
In reverence she held with pleasure
The lovely poems she possessed.

Bound in leather; bound together
within that textured maroon hide;
golden verse encased in gold-leaf,
honoured, treasured and sanctified.

Liquid language 'neath the cover,
rhyme and rhythm running free,
rends her heart, a verse-filled lover
vowing devoted constancy.

Locked within this timeless moment,
lost in blissful reverie,
she forgot that time was urgent,
kept open her anthology.

Cast adrift was fretful speeding
of hours which she could not possess;
work undone? She was not heeding,
soothed by a poet's fine caress.

THE FEEDER

A plump woodpigeon lands on the fence;
a blue-grey guy with a gimlet eye;
he unfolds his wings, his length immense,
plotting his path to the tree nearby.
Its bare branches hold a small bird's loot
of winter seeds in a tight mesh flute.

Up our bird loops, embracing the sky,
all wings and wobble flailing the air,
lands on a long twig, quite insecure;
but the goal is there – a stretch of the neck,
a claw on the mesh, a hasty peck …

… but no …

His bill is too big, the gaps too small,
off he lumbers, those small birds call!

ROMANCE IS IN THE AIR

Guests arrive, jump and jive or country dance –
Across the roof

Beneath the host glances; no, not a ghost,
foxtrot is proof

Here a peck, there a skip, quick wings a-flip,
claws loud and slick

Then squawks of romance, a busy brief chance –
possible chick?

X-rated gulls fly, tails up in the sky,
no time to brood

Young mottled brown bird? Oh, you have my word!
This will hold good

This fledgling will land, a pantomime grand
to get food quick!

So, what will appear the following year?
Another chick trick!

CUMBRIA

ODE TO EARLY SUMMER OF A DISUSED RAILWAY

I can slowly walk the rail track
and listen with a thrill
to the chubby chiffchaff chafing,
or restless willow warbler's trill.

Perhaps in smiling sunshine
a whitethroat may soar in play,
spot my clumsy, human movement,
cry alarm, drop, hide away.

Now buttercups and clover
spill wild heaven at my feet
while blissful in pale beauty
the hawthorn's scent wafts sweet.

It lures the passing insects,
enraptured by this tree;
I detect a fly-crammed bill,
the yellowhammer watches me.

In the valley of the railway,
grassy banks rise either side;
in gratitude I ramble
where tired miners once would ride.

A delight of untamed beauty,
no smooth cultivation here,
country treasures born of disuse
make a haven I hold dear.

UK

THE LITTLE MONSTER (OR TYPIST'S LAMENT)

There it sits, an
innocent thing
it seems …
until it starts to ring.

Every day,
I hope to be
caller-friendly
to folk phoning me.

In receptive mood
when work is light,
I plan my air
will be polite.

But there it sits …
it does not trill
in periods when
there's time to kill.

Instead it chooses
times of panic ...
with endless clanging ...
incessant ... manic.

I lose my cool ...
my friendly tone ...
good intentions
are quite blown!

It's a little monster
enacting burlesque,
feigned white innocence
upon my desk!

THE BLUE POT

In summer, leaf-cutter bees came
to the blue pot; made claim, bustled,
dug around its edges. Way down
they turned the soil. Above, a whirl
of tiny wings, a warning hum,
mouths full of bright shreds of green leaf.
Dumb I stand still, bewitched by bees
shaping their hidden nest, miners
designed by Nature; I felt blessed.

But when days became chill, they left.
Cruel, constant storms, reigned supreme, hope
fled, the blue pot sodden. Jaded,
I waited, berating Nature.
By mid June all hope had faded.

Then a boon – quick blurs of movement
play a magic fanfare of chance;
hope lifts as bees stir – they are there!
The whirl of young wings in the air.
Their dance of joy – dismay has fled –
a nest rebuilt with leafy shreds;
bees burrowing, quite unaware
they are blessed. That I care, I share
their presence on a beautiful day.

SPAIN

CICADA

The trees stand silent, no wind rustles dry leaves,
a dawn quietness settles on the wooded dell,
now the sun moves higher, orchestrates mystery,
touches quiet woods; Cicadas feel it, tune into
the conductor's baton as one, soar into
a stream of sound. Startling music answering
the sun; High symphonic soprano notes rise
loud and joyful, an embrace of insect life;
Big-eyed, gossamer winged, oscillating bugs,
a vast choir in perfect harmony, a grand
playing of slender violin legs. Then, a hush;
The music ceases; the symphony is over,
silent trees rest, dry leaves fall on clovered dell.

BLUE AND WHITE

From The Valley, a vision of shades
softening the fierce sun's reflection;
stripes cavorting in a gentle breeze,
splashes of colour on pale facades –
light-hearted, careless – they brightly wave
their frilled bold fringes of blue and white.

In the bustle of a cooling breeze,
heat shimmers, turns, slides towards
horizons, challenges the sea's shine,
glares at the jaunty, hillside colours;
terraces of pebbled white faces
nestling diamond-blue between the green.

(Homes built on the hillside in Calpe, Spain)

CLOUD CITY

October dawn colours the horizon
as heaven's artist begins her brush strokes;

caught in its glow, a cloud city appears;
beyond the edge, dense shapes hug the skyline
defining illusive bays, a sea-way
for ghost ships with foamy gossamer sails –

an ephemeral world which crumbles, fails –
flows into pale blue, shot through with scarlet.
Islands shift, drift, into a porous mass –
a vague wispy oblivion, blasted –

now a bright streak of sun – just a last hint
of haze to tell a citadel has fallen.

THE COMING OF COVID

A stillness haunts the silent roads,
no movement on the flat blue sea;
no tankers bearing heavy loads
can shake the water rising free

then fall; no cruise ships, layered, tall.

Silent beaches, smooth lonely sands,
No grainy castles, no child's glee,
moulding, shaping, with ice-cream hands;
no bustle for coffee or tea

no boys tossing balls carelessly.

The car parks are empty, stores too,
no business, no trading, no gain,
the world at a standstill, it's true!
An unknown disease starts it reign,

Harsh Covid Nineteen bludgeons through.

No place on earth can escape this,
No nation can now stand alone,
Join hands with blockage and deadness,
Weaken its power, bring it down.

This virus must be overthrown.

A CHRISTMAS DAY LAMENT

So, mother tripped up on my skateboard,
an endeavour I cannot believe!
'cos held in her hands was the turkey –
It flew, letting fat scorch my sleeve!

The pan did a bounce into mother,
who uttered two words lacking charm!
The turkey, meanwhile, had floored father,
and I had a scalded left arm!

So, here we are at the workhouse –
oh, hospital then if you must –
father's big toe is now bandaged,
and mother's uncomfortably trussed.

Yes, I am feeling quite gutted,
my arm, soaked in balm makes me fuss,
while the nurses eye us and snigger,
'Look at them!' … I silently cuss!

The three of us sit in the canteen,
wise men and one woman we're not,
wondering if puss has the turkey –
Happy Christmas, I almost forgot!

UK

ENTER A POET

Long ago in a far off land,
a stranger took me by the hand
Did I cry 'lay off, unhand me'?
I did not … nor saw a glittering eye!
Was I bewitched? Oh, joy, indeed!
A heart quite captured, spirit freed;
verse, sweet verse, played out on paper …
lost souls at sea, a ghostly vapour …

Oh poet, how I love thee,
your voice filled me with ecstasy
I made that journey, felt that fear
a dot, a mist, a speck, I wist;
It was my muse! Her hand I kissed
Long awakened, my words run free,
my pen a partner ever near;
… so came that day so long ago
when Coleridge whispered, 'Now you know!'

SERENADE

Nightingale with the most joyous of songs
sings for me this morn

her soaring notes fly, played to the pale dawn
bright, high, roundelay:

Trebles, warbles, full stops and crescendos
spring into the air

sleep banished, I wake to fair enchantment,
a flute of birdsong

I must follow each note, bewitched by a
little brown piper

THE MOUSE

At first his little nose peeped out;
The whisker-twitching little snout
was followed by black eyes, small and bright,
and soft brown body: He poised for flight –
listened; one slight noise would make it clear
there was something there for him to fear.
But ... silence ... there was no one to care
that a small, brown, furry mouse was there!

Leaving the safety of his home,
with nervous skip came out to roam.
He stood on hind legs and looked around;
He dropped down and sped across the ground;
But I must have moved; I saw that nose
twitch, once, twice, thrice and then he froze;
Next, faster than I had time to see,
he turned on his tail so rapidly;
Behind the tool shed, quite out of sight,
He'll bide now till the quiet of night.

FRANCE

ESPIRA FIRS

Green Indians stand on the hill,
Arms raised, without threat to the air;
Proud, still and straight,
They wait; ever there –
Through the centuries,
Watching our evolving valley.

Ancient man traced The Valley, found
A hidden plain, untouched, fertile;
Village stone masons,
Tillers of rich ground;
Here they built and farmed,
Spreading the grains of survival.

Today I live within history,
A modern arrival, I glance
Through my new window;
By chance I look up,
See high green Indians,
Sage, knowing and wise
To life's ongoing mystery.

TURKS AND CAICOS ISLAND

GIRL ON THE BEACH

I see the hut, its weathered state
a focus for an artist's eye;
worn and brown amid white-gold sand,
a shape to break blue sea and sky.

Windowless, it has no door, yet
a form glides out wild-tressed and fair,
walks from the hut on sandy floor –
no still life this, a girl is there

a tawny girl with yellow hair;
I watch that hut – that lass in mind
on silky sand, 'neath bright, clear skies.
A mystery of a travelling kind.

She stays there still, this lonely girl,
a coffee pot, a driftwood fire,
at home on sands where waves unfurl
and fish are grilled on rusted wire.

See … where the foam broils … there she stands,
an unclothed shape in froth and foam,
towel on the beach, soap in her hand;
salt-tangled hair she cannot comb.

But, time will heal, an altered scene …
it was the sea that brought her home;
behold her spirit, pure and clean,
a new life waits, no more she'll roam.

Today that hut is quiet and still
Bright curtains gone; an artist's scene!
His brush will catch the white foam's spill
while turquoise melts towards sea-green.

LONDON

7 JULY 2005

Yet again the greyness came;
vaporous and creeping,
smothering all the colours,
bursting out of the blue;
yellow falling into green and fading,
orange seeping into red;
a shame of prisms shattered,
atoms torn and bleeding;
blind degradation.

                             Horror

that unnatural light,
dark dread;
black dust, white faces;

                             Bombs

the disintegrating spaces;
and then
too much red;

and the *why* of it all;
the *why* of fanatics;
schemers who scatter the arcing
rainbow colours of nations;
sightless, senseless sages,
dreaming with us
from our beginning.
There, here, then, now;
the never-ending flag;
life-shattering idealism;
through the ages
onwards they soldier
in triumph's name.
A devil's game.

UK

HEAD OVER HEELS

I was fine with memory, nine out of ten,
but when was that …? How did a sneaky brat
called 'eighty-odd' fiddle with my mind? So
unkind! It's 'you know who', 'thingamibob';
my head throbs at Fred or Jane … and the same
for places; I recollect vague traces …

"She comes from somewhere north," I hear me say
while I mutely pray *please head, remember* …

an ember will do! Just a small trigger?
That unkind brat called eight-O whispers 'no!'
and the list grows as the grey cells scatter;
mind over matter? In vagueness the reverse!

The situ gets worse; a world of 'forgets' …
'whom have I told, whom have I not' figures,
becomes 'Oh, have I told you already?' …
A steady decline? No! Stop right there!
Have a care, head, renegotiate fate,
now what was I saying? Thoughts, please play fair!

ENLIGHTENMENT

'Tis God who gave life to man,
and Adam gave life to Eve
with his rib;
but I must crib,
for this I might not believe.

'Reason' doubts innate ideas
of Creation can hold true:
I am I think,
a natural link
of a million years ago.

And yet we do have feelings:
a mysterious heartfelt sense
lies in each breast:
a further test
of 'Reason' against 'Romance'.

Now speaks empirical Thought:

'out myth and superstition!'
'Science must be';
it moulded me
from fiery nuclear fission.

So … was man just a fireball?
Was God a glorious star?
Did man crash
as specks of ash?
Has Reason moved so far?

Who knows if God's in Heaven;
who knows if Adam is there,
and Eve of old
with hair of gold.
What pure truth can we declare!

DEVON

WILD GEESE AT DAWN

A streak of light, just a glimpse, a promise,
catches my eye, a brief glow; I listen …

hopeful for sound … a hint of muted
wings as the dawn sky tints the fading night.

A plaintive call, I hear it on the breeze,
crisp, beautiful, music as wings stir, sighing

into formation, the murmur of flight
as the gloom flees. High on the quick sun's tail

the day breaks free, heightens the symmetry
of a faultless vee, and the lake awaits.

THE ARRIVAL

The sun above the grey rooftops offers
a wan effort, a weary whine of *must I?*
The still, colourless sea is not impressed,
dressed in a sombre hue, it glances
upwards as it contemplates its chances
of a bright aspect; the seagulls collect
on tiles, clatter, chatter in raucous din,
then *light* lifts them, sends them winging to shore;

A golden blaze, free of cloud, dressed to please,
sparkles on the white froth, the wave shimmers,
lets a rolling sea catch it, turn it blue.
Will *light* stay? Is it Spring? The winds retreat
with a slight sigh of regret; they gather
their blustery chills, depart; trees are still:
Under the soil the miracle begins;
awakened, the seeds stir, twiglets bear buds.

Never a fair player, Winter sends forth
final grumbling blasts; a last cold trumpet
slides away, ebbing north; change skips in, sweeps
aside weak hues; bold strokes of blue survive
as the tide turns, and earth shows its palette:
Green leaves shelter paintbox colours; Pansies,
Crocus, yellow Daffodils weave wonder,
hope, and a promise that Spring will arrive.

SPIDER WORT

My interest is caught by a spider wort,
If you can believe it
Dark purple in hue, plain, this is true,
One takes it or leaves it
It creeps, it gets strong, its leaves form a throng,
Can you perceive it?
Fine hairs to ensnare some minuscule dot,
I like this a lot!
Delight in tips where leaves open their lips
And colour appears
Lilac in shade, a floral parade and
Small, dainty flowers –
Not plain at all, my attention is sought,
I watch wort for hours
It likes me as well, oh, this I can tell,
A petal plethora
Perhaps you think 'sad', consider me mad,
I simply adore her!

THE BURROWS

Freely I walk on The Burrows,
the furrows under my boots, soft,
yielding, clinging, mud on ridged
soles soon discarded in puddles;
A March landscape; as yet the spring sun
does not warm the soil, or wild grass –
a hard wind stings, passes quickly;
its prickly fingers scratch my eyes,
impeding vision. I linger
under grey skies; ahead huddled
sheep graze beside gentle horses
unfazed by chill forces of air;
I move forward, slow in motion,
voice a gentle flow of sound;
a mare turns, white and tan, looks, comes
towards me, bends her head for touch;
such joy, such trust; the horse moves on;
and so do I, glad I am here
within this set frame; this moment
is mine to keep, to take anywhere.